FROG

Watts Books
96 Leonard Street
London
EC2A 4RH

Franklin Watts Australia
14 Mars Road
Lane Cove
NSW 2066

ISBN 0 86313 693 1 (hardback)
ISBN 0 7496 1413 7 (paperback)

10 9 8 7 6 5 4 3 2 1

Paperback edition 1993

Design: Ben White

Printed in Italy by G. Canale & C. SpA

KEEPING MINIBEASTS

FROGS

TEXT: CHRIS HENWOOD

PHOTOGRAPHS: BARRIE WATTS

CONTENTS

What are frogs?.................6

Habitats.............................8

Collecting frogs and eggs..10

Handling.........................12

Housing for eggs and
    tadpoles.....................14

A simple pond 16

A special house...............18

Diet for a frog..................20

Breeding 22

Tadpole to froglet.............24

Releasing your frog 26

Unusual facts 28

Index 29

WATTS BOOKS

LONDON • NEW YORK • SYDNEY

Frogs are known as amphibians. This means that they can move and breathe on land as well as in water. Frogs usually spend part of their lives on land and part in water. All amphibians, including frogs, are cold-blooded.

This means that the animal has a temperature that is similar to its surroundings. So, if a frog is in a cold place it will be cold to touch. If it is in a warm place it will be warm to touch.

Habitats

There are more than 2000 different kinds of frogs. Only three kinds are found in Britain but over 90 kinds are found in North America. Some frogs live in ponds, lakes, streams and marshes. Others come from tropical forests

and even deserts. Some are found in different countries. Others come from only one place. Some frogs even live inside plants.

Collecting frogs

Frogs can sometimes be collected from the wild. But they are becoming endangered, so you may find that you are not allowed to collect adult frogs. You are usually allowed to collect some eggs, called spawn.

Collect only a very small amount of spawn
from one place. Fish out a small amount from
a pond using a small fishing net. Put the
spawn and some pond water into a water-tight
container.

As frogs are short and fat and very slippery they are very difficult to handle. When handling frogs use wet hands, as hot hands can harm their delicate skin. You can use a strainer or a damp towel or cloth held very gently around the body.

With very small frogs like Tree Frogs it is easiest to cup your hands. A word of warning — although you can buy Arrow Frogs, these should never be handled with bare hands.

Housing

Different frogs need different housing. Some can be indoors, some can be outdoors. Tadpoles and young froglets could have a

tank lined with gravel, filled with water and weeds. Add a small rock so the froglet can climb out of the water. For older frogs use a fish tank with about a third water area and two thirds land area.

A simple pond

If you want to keep frogs outdoors you can start in a very simple way. You can make your own pond — if your family agrees!

You will need a plastic bowl, a small strainer and some plants.

Find a fairly shady plot of ground. Dig a hole and place the plastic bowl in it. Fill the bowl with water and put plants around and in it.

Keep your eyes open for frogs if you visit someone with a large garden pond.

A special house

A tank like this is called a vivarium. It is usually only needed to house "exotic" frogs, for example Tree Frogs.

It is a tall tank with growing plants, heat and a special light. It needs only a small water area but the whole tank should be sprayed inside with water once a day.

Diet for a frog

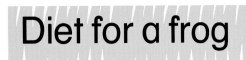

Different types of frogs need different types of food. All frogs have one thing in common. They all like to eat moving prey – that means they eat other animals.

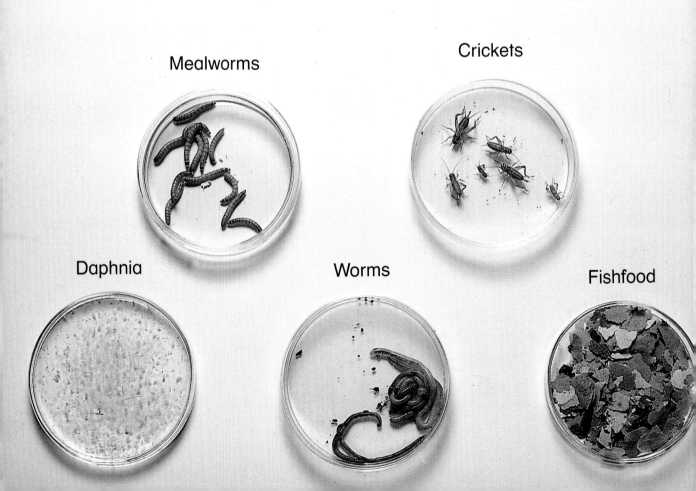

Mealworms

Crickets

Daphnia

Worms

Fishfood

Young frogs will eat water fleas (daphnia) and water insects.

Older frogs will eat various types of food including mealworms, earthworms, slugs, snails, moths, locusts, flies and caterpillars.

Breeding

Most frogs lay their eggs in water. The breeding season usually starts early in spring as the weather begins to get warmer.

The eggs are laid by the female in the water. They are then fertilized by the male. The frogs' eggs (called spawn) look like black pinheads in clear jelly.

Tadpoles feed off the jelly which protects them. They hatch after about ten days and should then be given pond algae, weeds or small pieces of lettuce.

When the tadpoles have grown legs they will want to leave the water. Place some rocks in the tank and as the froglets spend more time on the rocks move them to a land-based vivarium.

You can let your frogs go back into the pond where you collected the eggs, or you may use them to restock ponds.

Never release frogs that are not native to your area into the wild. You could upset the balance of your local wildlife and the "exotic" frogs will probably die.

Frogs drink through their skin.

The average jump for a common frog is 600mm (24 in) or 6 to 7 times its own body length.

A frog's tongue can extend 10mm (½ in) from the mouth.

The African Clawed Frog has no tongue and never leaves the water in its life.

The Water Holding Frog of Australia spends most of its life in an earth burrow waiting for the very rare rains to enable it to breed.

The Barking Frog is so called because its mating call sounds like the barking of a dog.

Index

African Clawed Frog 28
amphibians 6
Arrow Frog 13
average jump 28

Barking Frog 28
breeding 22, 23
breeding season 22

eggs 10, 22, 23, 27

female 23
fishing net 11
froglets 14, 25

habitats 8, 9
handling frogs 12, 13

insects 21

male 23

pond 8, 16, 17
pond algae 24
releasing frogs 27
restocking ponds 27

spawn 10, 11, 23
spring 22

tadpoles 14, 24, 25
tank 18
Tree Frog 13, 18

vivarium 18, 25

Water Holding Frog 28
worms 21